POEMS AND TRAN-QUILITY

Ikugbayigbe Paul O

Poems and Tranquility

Paul I

Published by Paul I, 2021.

POEMS AND TRANQUILITY

First edition. July 31, 2021.

Written by Paul I.

To God Almighty, my Creator.

POEM ONE: THE POWER OF LOVE

That love,
The love from you,
Agape love,
Your own love
Show me the grace
That I love,
As you do,
The Power,
The great power,
Of that love,
God's kind of love
It's what we need
Show me your love,
That righteous love,
That holy love,
Teach it to me,
Show it to me,
The power of love,
Only you,
Can give
Show me your love,
That I love rightly
With desires forsaken
Give me
The power to win
Give me

The power of love
That love
Without blemish
Without stains
Pure and whole
Lord of lords
Give me from above
The power of love.

POEM TWO: ANYTHING IS POSSIBLE

Yes
Everything
Anything
It is possible
If you make it possible
So
Anything is possible
Yeah
It seems impossible
Yes it is possible
For who makes it possible
Who creates possibilities?
No one
No other one but him
It is him
The great creator
Yes
He makes all things possible
So I believe
I know
I feel
That anything is possible.

POEM THREE: IT IS LAZINESS

Poverty come
    He screams
    Misery stop
    He cries
    Laziness
    Faith of poverty
    Brother of pain
    Master of misery
    Laziness
    The virtue
    That brings one from grass to grace
    Enemy of hard work
    Servant of insufficiency
    Of sadness
    Even weeping
    Sorrow
    All given in a bowl
    Oh
    Run away
    From his dirty claws
    He who harms without pity
    And kill without mercy
    Laziness
    For how long
    Shall you rule
    In the evil place?
    Friends

Of all your choices
Yes
All your decisions
Never pick laziness
That demon
That monstrosity
For that will be
The worst of all decisions.

POEM FOUR: OLD DEAD WOODS

When they are young
    Tending to cheat
    Even to steal
    Some tried to kill
    But their doom waits
    Their woes await
    Waiting for them
    To walk in
    Yes
    They say
    We have done no evil
    We have done no harm
    But woe to their victim
    How I pity their prey
    Now is the time
    For them to suffer for their deeds
    Now they are old
    Old dead woods
    Yes
    Now they live a life
    Of sorrow and regret
    Some in prison
    Few are dead
    But the ones who still live
    Feel the agony and pain
    But now

They are old woods
Old dead woods.

POEM FIVE: AT THE EXTREME

Standing
    On the edge
    So close to the sea
    Just a step
    And he is in
    Close to that state
    Of being in numbness
    Yet nothing
    Virtually nothing
    Nothing except the Creator intervenes
    Can stop him
    From closing in
    A painful closeness
    Almost like a friend
    To depression and anxiety
    At the extreme
    It feels like you are out
    Of all types of agonies
    Of all types of pains
    The one I dread most of all,
    Is being at the extreme
    For just a step
    A little step
    He is away
    From the wrist of hell
    Even death
    The worst I say

The worst of all
Is being at the extreme.

POEM SIX: PATIENCE

Yes
A while
Just a while
The breakthrough occurs
I wish it
Yes
To happen right now
For the confusion
The agony
But weeping may endure for a night
Yet joy comes in the morning
Slowly but steadily
Our frown becomes a smile
Our anger turns to gladness
Yes even our hate turns to love
And then we praise the Creator
But imagine
Just imagine
Disappointment smiled again
Then impatience moves on
Anger gets more space
And soon we drift
Away
And away from the Creator
Till we are far away
Yea
Very far

And then we try to pray
All in vain
My God
My Lord
I cling to you
Show me your patience
Give me your patient spirit
I cry unto you
Lead me not astray
Yes
I lay my heart in you bosom
Yes
I shall be patient.

POEM SEVEN: THE LORDS PRAYER

Our father
>Who art in heaven
>Hallowed be your holy name
>Yes
>On the mouth of the sinners and criminals
>It abounds like flowing waters
>They say it
>But do they mean it?
>Thy great kingdom come
>Thy will be done on earth
>As it is in heaven
>We say it
>Yes we do
>Ask him
>Of proverbs 23
>Or the Lord's Prayer
>And what does he choose
>Do not be surprised
>For the Lord's Prayer
>Has it not become?
>The *common prayer*
>For even the murderers say it
>No
>It is not
>For the creator is forgiving
>So

Give us this day
Our daily bread
And forgive us our trespasses
Just as we forgive those who trespass against us
Lord; lead us not into temptation
But deliver us from all evils
For you is the kingdom
All power and glory
Forever and ever

POEM EIGHT: THAT LIFE OF CONFUSION

Standing
    On the verge of falling
    With not an iota of hope
    All thoughts of help are dashed
    They are in shambles
    In pieces
    With a life as that
    Of a convicted felon
    Shattered into pieces
    As greased up
    Even as old weary dress
    And yet
    Still stepped on
    Changed in seconds
    From stones
    To dust
    Not until the creator intervenes
    It is a painful life
    A life of confusion
    Not knowing the left
    Or even the right
    All this occur
    In that shameful life
    That life of confusion.

POEM NINE: FEAR

Looking around
    Trembling inside
    Shaking
    Feeling scared
    Of all things
    Fear is the creepiest
    The creepiest of all
    Coming like a thief
    Leaving like a king
    Fear
    The sorrowful one
    The demon
    Fear
    Sneaky at first
    But when he sees that boldness is not around
    And courage is not near
    He walks in
    As majestically as a governor
    Fear
    The one
    That causes men to shake
    Fear
    The one with claws
    Claws as that of a lion
    Fear
    The one that tries
    To wipe out before he leaves

Not leaving a remnant
Nor even a trail.

POEM TEN: LOVE

The strong feeling
Touching through
Right through the heart
Love
So beautiful
Gentle and calm
Serene as night
Love
The successor of affection
The mind blowing angel
That brings peace
True peace
Even happiness
Love
Brother of kindness
Friend of hospitality
Love
A servant of the Mighty One
Sent by him
To guide our hearts
Love
Take heed
For the day is come
When the shadows of hatred
Shall try its best to triumph over you
But the Mighty One
Who rules all things

Shall defeat it
And you shall reign again
All people
Let thy gates be opened
For love to enter
Love
The master of all good things
You are honored
As a part
An attribute
Of the Mighty One
All people
All people on earth
Take heed
And have love!

POEM ELEVEN: ALL I WANT IS YOU

You give me joy
 You make me happy
 Only you can touch my soul
 All I want is you
 You my creator
 You my God and king
 Yes
 I ask; who is like you?
 Who can liken himself as you?
 You
 You that make my soul to swell with emotions
 My heart to burst with your love
 No
 It is only you
 And all I want is you.

POEM TWELVE: THE SONG OF THE BIRDS

Your song
    It is like sweet melody
    It feels like harmony
    Your songs sound like special honey
    It soothes the ear like a balm
    It brings ease
    The song of the birds
    No song can compare to that song
    It softens the deepest anger
    It weakens the strongest mortal
    It fills the hungriest men
    It turns stone into dust
    The song of the birds
    Composed by the Creator
    The greatest song of all
    When man sings
    Tears drop
    When you sing
    Men weep like babies
    You song
    It make a demon repent
    It makes a criminal surrender
    It's your song
    The song of the birds.

POEM THIRTEEN: BEFORE DAYBREAK

Dawn shall arrive
    Hear the crow's shill cry
    Yea
    It comes
    Dusk has come
    Life is still
    Nature is quilled
    Then the Creator speaks
    And behold, day
    The sweet dark sky
    The small white stars
    But for some lives begin at night
    And alas, daybreak!
    For day shall come
    For days shall pass
    We shall wait
    And the day comes
    The sun shines
    Yes
    The day is near.

POEM FOURTEEN: THE PUZZLE OF LIFE

Scattered
Shattered
Smattered
Battered
One is well dressed
One wears rags
One ride cars
One wants bikes
For is not the rich man happy?
Is not the poor man sad?
No
The rich man gets sadder
He believes he is getting poorer
The ironies of life
The impossible puzzle
The unsolvable puzzle
While some hustle and battle
Others lay on couches
When some eat as chickens
Others feed like hawks
Life
It is an irony
As bendy as a path
As wary as a curve
Truly life is not balanced.

POEM FIFTEEN: THE CRY FROM ABOVE

From the sky
    Then come the cry
    Brittle and spry
    Loud
    Like the roar of a lion
    Great
    Like the trumpet of an elephant
    The cry from the sky
    The cry of justice
    The cry of love
    Piercing through the coldest hearts
    Touching even the dullest minds
    The wail
    The sorrow
    The cry of the sky
    For the pains
    The shame
    The hate
    The vengeance
    It is the cry of sadness
    Yet a cry of joy
    A cry of disappointment
    Yet a cry of happiness
    Happy for tomorrow
    The future
    It is filled with hope

Happy for us all
It comes down like a scream
It leaves like a whisper
Yes
The day of peace comes
The day of love comes
Then the cry from above shall prevail.

POEM SIXTEEN: CONSECRATED FOR YOU

I am for you Lord
    Only you
    You only
    The most high
    Your voice
    Like the wailing thunder
    Your steps
    Like earthquakes
    Lord
    I want to be for you
    I am for you
    No one but you
    You are my alpha
    You are my very soul
    I put my life in your hands
    I want to be for you
    I cling to your hem
    I hold on to your feet
    Take me as your own
    Make me as your own
    You I trust
    To make my spirit whole.

POEM SEVENTEEN: AGAPE LOVE

God's chosen
>The creator's own
>The love from above
>Agape love
>God's kind of love
>That love
>Hot as burning embers
>Strong
>Resilient
>Determined
>Pure
>The love of the most high
>That love
>Sweet sugar
>It is true love
>Pure
>The love of the most high
>That love
>Sweet as sugar
>It is true love
>It is not fantasy
>Neither is it ecstasy
>It is only from the source
>It is the love of the Lord.

POEM EIGHTEEN: HE LIVES IN ME

He dwells in my heart
    He reigns in me
    He has his place
    A special place
    He makes me
    He gives me boldness
    Courage
    Power
    Life
    You reign
    It is you
    The ancient of days
    Yes
    You are in me
    As I am in you
    The one that gives life
    I hold onto you
    You Lord reign in me
    In us
    You Lord
    You contract my heart
    You guard will all jealousy.

POEM NINETEEN: IT IS WHO YOU ARE

It is you
>The Lord of all
>When you speak
>Mountains rumble
>The sky sings your praise
>The birds worship you the trees bow before you
>The stones scream your glory
>It is who you are
>It is what you are
>You are invisible
>Omnipotent
>Omnipresent
>The omniscience
>I bow before you
>Your throne of glory shows your might
>Is it not you?
>You that holds the earth with a finger
>You that carry our burdens like a feather
>No
>You live forever
>The eternal one
>Our creator
>It is who you are.

POEM TWENTY: THE SPIRIT OF PATIENCE
You walk the earth with ease
You thread our hearts with glory
It is y
Servant of the Creator
You that makes the righteous better
You make the foolish wise
You make the wise wiser
You soften the hardest heart in a flash
You are magnificent in your own splendor
You bring the most downcast up
You make the weak strong
You change the heart of a villain
And bless the mind of the truthful
You are great
Greater than truth
Subtler than Pains and Hate
You are *patience*.

POEM TWENTY-ONE: A STITCH IN TIME

Not one
    Neither two
    The afore hand place
    The prevention
    A stitch in time
    The stitch in time
    Saves nine
    Is it not better?
    To stop it before it begins
    To quell it before it overpowers
    To quash it before it crushes
    Is it not better?
    To prevent than to cure
    To protect than to heal
    Yes
    Is not it a factor of patience?
    Is not it a follower of calmness?
    It is
    Truly it is
    It tell you
    I believe
    And I shall always believe
    That a stitch in time saves life.

POEM TWENTY-TWO: WHEN IS SEEMS IMPOSSIBLE

Then the Creator smiled
    The trees laughed
    Truth danced
    And it was made a possibility
    Yes
    For life is an impossibility
    For how did the Creator make man from dust?
    Or how did the father make the organs
    No
    No one knows
    How impossibilities came into life
    Or how possibilities stepped into a cold corner
    Life was brought
    Mercy replaced reality
    Truth replaced impossibilities
    Yes
    Possibility took its place
    And life was renewed
    The Lord said it was possible
    Reality laughed until he gasped
    Fear rasped and gasped
    Fear rasped and gasped
    All over he smiled
    No,
    Reality doused ability
    Possibility woke magnanimity

Then the creator appeared
Peace was restored
On reality was bestowed
The supernatural abilities of possibility
Then possibilities stone like stars
Opportunities flew around like butterflies
His power was revealed
Life was rekindled
His strength was displayed
And reality become possibility
Yes
Possibility was reality.

POEM TWENTY-THREE: A NEW DAWN

Fresh as the air
  Beautiful as the morning star
  A dawn comes
  The day has dawned
  The time has come
  The lust long gone
  The new era has just begun
  Cause life itself has just been born
  Yes
  Truthfulness and holiness
  Meekness and righteousness
  Perfection abounds
  A match towards happiness
  A step towards brighter days
  Great peace the future holds
  Now is the time
  For a new dawn.

POEM TWENTY-FOUR: NIGERIA (WITH CONCEPT BY IKUBAYIGBE NIMOROTI)

A nation of fashioned wonder
A Land of unequalled wonder
The home of natural beauty
The heart of Africa
Center of the west
The pace setter of the southern wield
The giant of the African continent
We are Nigeria
We are one
May the Creator bless our nation
From the Niger to the coast
From the savannahs to the valleys
A land of milk and honey
The land of love and honor
Yet who sits at the outskirts?
It is he, impatience
Is not that corruption?
And hatred too
Yes
But when the Creator intervenes
Then shall the deliverer be known.

POEM TWENTY-FIVE: THE SILENT WEEPING HEART

Happy on the outside
Smiling and chortling
Yet weeping on the inside
Wailing
Bawling
For you
That is the price to pay
Your price to pay
Yes
You believe it is your lot
That it dwells in your living
It is part of your destiny
But no
For the Creator wishes you prosperity
Physically and mentally
Yes,
He does
He is the Master
Yet he shares in your pains
He is steady when others get heady
When your brain gets stuffy
He makes you feel cozy
Cozy in his warm embrace
His lovely embrace.

POEM TWENTY-SIX: THE SAINT STORY

Yes
　　Holy and just
　　True and loving
　　Servants of the most high
　　The saints
　　The holies
　　The truthful
　　The Grateful
　　Patience revers them
　　Truth abounds in them
　　Gladness is fulfilled in them
　　Goodness lives in them
　　Some of you martyrs
　　Your sacrifice duly rewarded
　　With eternal living
　　They were beaten
　　Some injured
　　Stabbed
　　Murdered
　　They were beaten
　　Some injured
　　Stabbed
　　Murdered
　　It is their story
　　Their reward from the creator
　　Waits for them in heaven.

POEM TWENTY-SEVEN: THE ARRANGED SPIRIT

Yes
    In the right way
    It is realism
    The sorted heart
    The orderly life
    Saintly arrangements
    Truthful and orderly
    Neat and arranged
    Clear and in the exact way
    An attraction of values
    The epitome of diligence
    A storehouse of hard work
    A cupboard of truth
    Yes
    The realist's spirit
    A believer of orderliness
    Home of cleanliness
    A life of happiness awaits such a being.

POEM TWENTY- EIGHT: PEACE LIKE A RIVER

Happiness glowing
   Destines shining
   Lives brimming
   Cause peace is flowing
   Yes
   True peace
   Peace like a river
   Flowing like a river
   I have peace like a river
   Deep in my soul
   Giving me happiness
   Gladness
   Truthfulness
   The feeling of true love
   Yes
   Peace
   It is wonderful
   Saves me from a storm
   Keeps me from all troubles
   The Creator gives me peace
   He is *true* peace

POEM THIRTY-THREE: THE DEMON CALLED DEATH

Dedicated to **ADEBAWALE SAMUEL P**, lead compiler of the defunct edition of "Ten fishes you must know" Born 2007 and died 2020.

Death
That monstrosity
That evil
How I hate you
You take away
What we love most
Steal away
What we cherish
Why?
Why do you steal our beloved?
Are you sad?
Are you vengeful?
But I know
That all shall fall into you trap
The choice they make
Determines their lot
Yea
You are of the devil
You are truly evil
But one thing I knew
Is that the creator shall avenge.

POEM THIRTY: HIS IMMEASURABLE LOVE

His love for me
    Cannot be compared
    Can only be revered
    He loves me
    I cannot tell why
    Only he can love me like he does
    His immeasurable love
    His unquantifiable love
    Unconditional love
    His love
    So great
    Not matched by any other
    I am driven with the passion
    To cry before you
    To lay down in your comfort
    To stand in your presence
    There is none but you
    None like you
    You are the mighty rock
    The prince of all
    How I cherish your love.

POEM THIRTY-ONE: THE STORM IS COMING

A storm shall begin
   In the final moment
   The last times
   It might not subside
   A great storm it shall be
   Raging like thunder
   Wild as tornadoes
   Strong as bison
   It shall come
   It will come
   Shaking the earth
   Pondering all life
   No happy moments it will bring
   But sorrow and pain
   They shall be seen
   Then that moment
   All love and care
   Happiness and joy
   Away to the sky they shall go
   Nevertheless
   I will be ready.

POEM THIRTY- TWO: FROM GRASS TO GRACE

From grass to grace
    It sounds in no way right
    But grace to grass
    Yes
    That sound real
    But we all know
    The best of all
    It is grass to grace
    Yes
    For man would rather rise
    From poor to rich
    Than fall
    From rich to poor
    So to the Creator I pray
    That the reverse be the case
    That I shall differ
    Grass to grace
    Rising
    Ascending
    From slave to master
    From servant to master
    Yes
    We may all remain
    The servants of the creator
    But here on earth?
    Some slave under their fellow beings.

POEM THIRTY-THREE: HOLDING MY HEART

In his very hands
My heart rests in
My life dwells on
Your love makes me swell
In your presence I dwell
Only you
Can take my life
And makes it into something new
You mold my heart like clay in a potter's hand
Whenever you are close
I feel like I am in love
In love with your person
In love with your goodness
In love with you
Yes
I am armored by your splendor
Engulfed in your worship
I kneel before your throne
You my creator
You that make heaven and earth
In you all things are made reality
Under you
Reality is glad
Happiness resides
Truthfulness decides
Obedience beside

Your strike like the melting stone
You reign as the king of all
Only you
Can hold my heart.

POEM THIRTY-FOUR: MY MOTHER (DEDICATED TO MRS MOJISOLA IKUGBAYIGBE THE BEST MOTHER OF ALL)

He brilliant eyes sparkle
When she smiles
Her pretty face radiates love
It shows peace
She raises my sprit when I am down
I love her very much
Yes I do
It is she
Who bathed me
Who nursed me
Who grew me
Who chastised me
Who cared for me
It is she
That supports me?
Cherishes me
When she speaks to me
My soul is raised
When she chastises me
My heart jumps for joy
How good it is
To have a caring mother.

POEM THIRTY-FIVE: A FATHER'S LOVE (DEDICATED TO MR TOMOLOJU IKUBAYIGBE AND ALL MEN AROUND THE WORLD)

Cuddling me
Holding me
A father does that
On the eve of the birth
He sits like a king
Smiling proudly
He is now a father
He watches me grow
Supports me in every way
Loves me in many forms
Through stern at times
Strict at times
His love for me
Never fades
Yes
He has his weakness
Yes
He has his pitfalls
But he will always stay strong
Like the father that he is.

POEM THIRTY-SIX: A FULFILLED DREAM

Hopes contained
  Doubt obtained
  Love retained
  Patience untamed
  The dream is reality
  Imagination is realization
  But you look around
  You see reality
  You see the dream
  Looking close
  You see hard work
  Strength
  Energy
  Pawn
  All for purpose
  Working for a reason
  Even destiny comes in
  Happiness stands close by
  The dream that all men would wish for
  The fulfilled dream.

POEM THIRTY-SEVEN: THE LIVING FIRE

Spreading
>Flowing
>Growing like an eagle
>Sprouting like a seed
>The living fire
>Hot as live coals
>Burning unconditionally
>The fire of life
>Powerful
>Mighty
>Burning as stars
>Who is the great fire?
>What is the great fire?
>It is no one else
>None but the Creator
>The lord of all things.

POEM THIRTY-EIGHT: OPEN THE FLOOD GATES

Open your mighty doors
    And let your rain fall
    Let it descend mightily
    Sprit of the most high
    Lord of all
    Pour down your blessings
    Show us your breakthrough
    Provide for us your children
    Show us your never ending mercy
    Your always burning love
    Tender hearted
    Mightier than a sword you are
    There is no one compared
    No one like you
    No man besides you
    In the heavens
    On the earth
    It is only you
    That has the key to the doors of blessing
    In your palm all true power
    All righteous wealth
    In the palm of your hands they lay.

POEM THIRTY-NINE: THE SHEPHERD'S PRAYER

Show me your steadfast love
Give me your mighty trust
Protect me with your graceful mercy
For you oh lord
Thou art my salvation
My peace and joy
The shepherd of all
Guide me in all my ways
Lead me in all my dealings
Show me the path of righteousness
Bestow on me
The mark of abundance
Unto you I pray
Oh lord
For guidance and protection
Cover me with your flowing blood
Willing to you savior of all
Show me your blessings and calm
Now shall you bestow on me
Your wonderful love and mercy
Deliver from evils of life
Save me from the hate of men
Amen.

POEM FOURTY: THE JUDGEMENT DAY

The day shall come
The greatest day of all
The judgment day
When man shall stand before the creator
And sing or cry
Some will bow to him
Then their lot
They shall know
Whether damnation
Whether eternal joy
The choice shall be made
And the Word shall smile
Grace will grin all round
Love will shine like stars
Gladness shall laugh and dance
Then the truthful shall be chosen
Sanctified
Yes
The angels shall proliferate
On the last day
The judgment day.

ABOUT THE BOOK

This collection is loaded with love, faith, trust in God, even righteousness.

It is right for a bleeding heart or a broken soul. It is right for dynamic and mind-enlightening soul-lifting.

Welcome to the world of Poetic expressions.

Paul Ikugbayigbe is a Nigerian. He lives at Abuja with his parents and sister. This is his first poetry work.

Also by Paul I

Poems and Tranquility

About the Author

Paul Ikugbayigbe is Nigerian. He lives in Abuja with his family.

About the Publisher